# Love Lingers

Poetry by
Linda Dominique Grosvenor

Published and Distributed in the United States

Cover Design: John Riddick, Jr.

Copyright ©2002 by Linda Dominique Grosvenor

All rights reserved. No part of this book may be reproduced in any form or by any means without the prior written consent of the Publisher, except brief quotes used in reviews.

Library of Congress Card Number: 2002105200

ISBN 0970010265 (pbk)

First Printing, January, 2002
10 9 8 7 6 5 4 3 2 1

Printed and Bound in the United States of America

www.LindaDominiqueGrosvenor.com

"we love because it's the only true adventure..."

-- Nikki Giovanni

# Acknowledgments

I'd like to thank my husband John, my family and friends, the Prolific Writers Network, and various other people and sources for inspiring poetry in me. I thank the world wide web for allowing me to tag my verse all over the place and God for whom without His truth, I would still be bowing down worshipping statues believing they can hear me.

**Dedication**

To those who loved and lost yet dared to love again

# Love Lingers

## Preface

*Herein lies every quirky, shy, private and uninhibited thought that I've had in reference to love over the past several years. Some thoughts are simple and others more enormous and complex, due to the fact that love is a really viable emotion that cannot be caged or limited to mere adjectives. I thank those of you in my life who were lovable enough to be rendered in poetry and also those who were not, for it is only in the not loving that we can define loving, thus distinguishing between the two. I perceive myself as blessed to have loved, lost and yet dare to love again. And although some naïve souls say that I'm too intense and tend to lay it on a bit thick, lose yourself in my words and allow them to erase some of your preconceived notions about me, yourself and someone you love. Allow the words to tear down the walls that surround you until they are low enough for someone to peel back the layers, see inside your heart and love you terribly.*

## Table of Contents

| | |
|---|---|
| Kiss | 10 |
| Croon | 11 |
| Ponder | 12 |
| Stay | 13 |
| Plum | 14 |
| Ramblings | 15 |
| Breasts | 16 |
| Shine | 17 |
| Hands | 18 |
| Chocolate | 19 |
| Prisoner | 20 |
| Missed | 21 |
| Virtue | 22 |
| Invited | 23 |
| Amoré | 24 |
| Showering | 25 |
| Vice | 26 |
| Who | 27 |
| Scorched | 28 |
| Flower | 29 |
| Sugar | 30 |
| Assume | 31 |
| Honey | 32 |
| Honeymoon | 33 |
| Livid | 34 |
| Accomplice | 35 |
| Joy | 36 |
| Fire | 37 |
| Dreams | 38 |
| Mail | 39 |
| Righteous | 40 |
| Vows | 41 |
| June | 42 |
| Ambiguity | 43 |
| Real | 44 |
| Never | 45 |
| Skin | 46 |
| Naked | 47 |
| When | 48 |
| Gypsy | 49 |
| Hot | 50 |
| Linger | 51 |
| Sea | 52 |
| Celebrate | 53 |
| Matilda | 54 |
| She | 55 |
| Extricate | 56 |
| Dance | 57 |
| Sunrise | 58 |
| Taxicab | 59 |
| Autumn | 60 |
| Introverted | 61 |
| Sleeping | 62 |
| Easy | 63 |
| Falling | 64 |
| Uncovered | 65 |
| Alibi | 66 |
| Wasted | 67 |
| Abstract | 68 |
| Remember | 69 |
| More | 70 |
| Everything | 71 |
| Chores | 72 |
| Naught | 73 |
| Jealousy | 74 |
| Jessy | 75 |
| Forbidden | 76 |
| If | 77 |
| Leaves | 78 |
| Midnight | 79 |
| Rain | 80 |
| Always | 81 |
| Sinful | 82 |
| Could | 83 |
| Fallen | 84 |
| Perfection | 85 |
| Suppose | 86 |
| Yearn | 87 |
| Kid | 88 |
| Facade | 89 |
| Caught | 90 |
| Spanish | 91 |
| Friday | 92 |
| Born | 93 |
| Baby | 94 |
| King | 95 |
| Magnets #3 | 96 |
| Music | 97 |
| Armed | 98 |
| Truth | 99 |
| Being | 100 |
| Misunderstood | 101 |
| Yesterday | 102 |
| Rejection | 103 |
| Free | 104 |
| Ransom | 105 |
| Toy | 106 |
| Seventeen | 107 |
| Coffee | 108 |
| Ode to Tim | 109 |

## Kiss

I kiss you like bruised fruit
too soft to handle well,
your flesh nudges, rapping timidly
like a missed curfew at half past 2.
Your lips lift me from my boyish shoes
liberating me into obscure femininity,
you peck me with flecks of speckled kisses
and the same tongue you sealed the letter
telling me good-bye.

## Croon

I want to play my guitar for you
strum a crooked song off key
whistle a virgin tune
cuddle you fast in my melody
while whetting the moon's appetite
for the sun, as I croon a sexy falsetto
masquerading in nonchalance
loving the devil out of you.

## Ponder

Breathless melodies cradle your remembrance
as I am nervously nudged by a ginger-skinned girl
to "please fasten my seatbelt."
I've relinquished my mental solitude
to what you scribbled in blue on ecru
a never feigning love is what you conveyed
your eyes held me, chin up, captive, applauding ditto.
But you're my remedy; I'm high on you
intoxicated, inhaling deeply, equilibrium off kilter,
sky forgiving, allowing me undaunted to lounge
in the fashion of your psychedelic lullabies.
There is more than echoing distance now,
there are seeds you've planted, as you grow on me
and I am as dutiful as honeydew melons with thick skin
and succulent flesh that gives itself as an offering.
Rain down your love; come drench my heart,
as I nourish the part of you that hungers for a taste.
Fill yourself on the fragrance of me,
allow me to cross your mind today.

## Stay

Serendipity and first kisses
near the soda machine,
but you call it "*pop.*"
Your lips traced mine as
my racing heart fights
to keep up with the
images coming undone in my mind.
One day in the vicinity of forever
we'll no longer keep an
eye out for departure signs
and express our exaggerated good-byes
in a damp airport with prying minds
but we'll seek something "for sale,"
that we can admirably mark "sold,"
with our "I Do."

*Linda Dominique Grosvenor*

## Plum

Yum, yum, I see thee
glistening, firm and dark,
drawing buzzing sounds
they hum and circle 'round unlearned
as I try to sit and ponder,
if it's better to bite
or touch, look, listen.
My fingers they press you,
caress you, undress you, skin first
leaving teeth prints deeper
as you find comfort near my lips,
telling me your zealous flesh
has never tasted sweeter than
the moment some of you
ran  down my chin.

## Ramblings

In a hallucinating moment he closed his eyes
and soaked in the words as though
it was the iridescent yellow of the sun.
So eloquent and cooperatively
it flowed together, musically.
Just speculation it could have been
but ravages calamity shall not confess,
idleness forgotten and melancholy twice denied
convinces him that in her poetry, love has no color.
So, he ate the words like grapes, picking them
from the vine of hunger, feeling only
a warm fuzzy softness, that was neither
scorned nor disproved.

## Breasts

Roaming eyes, a brush in passing
hands softly uncovering, slowly exposing
the excitement hidden within.
I hold them both for a verbal ransom
yet gladly surrender to lips in a truce.
How fair they are by the mirror's reflection
offering themselves in silence
as patience escapes us and
the quickened breath dares tell.
They sigh for you; they smile for you
they beckon you to come hither,
whispering touch and lips so sweet
the flicker of a tongue doth complete.

## Shine

You painted my life
with sunshine and forgetfulness
like a black and white movie
that I've only seen twice (*once with you*).
There is always a drab and dreary echoing
prompted by your absence
and a corridor with the lingering scent
of where you'd been just moments before.
Are you an invention of my loneliness?
Melting into the night
waiting for the dawn to drink you in
and spew you out as pulsing rays
that shine me on to my fate?
You made me your flower child and
freely gave me pieces of you to ponder,
your lips! your lips!
And our minds melded
as I felt your dreams
and you spoke my thoughts
prophetically into the wind.

## Hands

A treaty my body made with your hands
to give pleasure, to touch, subdue.
Wandering the contours of softly shaven me,
the warmth it exudes does exist, as we
dispute the rumor of the loveless earth.
Familiarity and tenderness, affection overdue
more that I could have imagined,
you are a reward for my patience
as you create in me, love, art and poetry.

## Chocolate

I imagine you're my rich cocoa flavor
as I stir you into the submission of my love.
The essence of you rolls off
the tip of my tongue and I
o v e r f l o w
for you my bittersweet
as your verbal freedom ponders us
in this two by two society that feeds the fire,
and I taste the richness of your masculinity
when it stands up for me and
takes no thought in laying me down.

## Prisoner

When you say "I want you,"
I lose myself absent-mindedly.
I believe I'm still captive
in our conversation from last night.
Why do you open me up so,
like a gaping wound, oozing
leaving me shivering, exposed
wide-eyed with my tail between my legs,
as you strip me down on the inside?
You take no prisoners, yet your words cuff me,
your love arrests me, and lets me off
with merely a warning:
that if I pass this way again
I could be head over heels by morning.

## Missed

So today I am missed.
The wafting scent of me
is relished until it no longer is.
A postcard, a letter
a love song on a cassette.
You close your eyes and imagine me,
lips moving slowly and pouting at times
in an almost deliberate fashion.
I'm trying hard to get my way.
I want to see what I'm capable of.
I'd like to leave you a reminder
of a girl who you met, but never knew
would change your life.
I want you to notice me
unarmed, as we speak — face to face,
enjoying the slight hum
of contentment that
emanates from our souls.

## Virtue

I'd like to dance to
the wind of your rhythm
and teeter on the edge of passion
that peels back
and reveals layers,
tasting honesty
and wrapping myself
in a bantering virtue
that need not wear a disguise.

## Invited

I feel gift-wrapped special
like a breeze that's been invited
a wind that seeks an undisturbed place
to twirl about and prance carelessly.
I possess a taste for adventure
in the cavalier sense of doing.
You left footprints on my heart,
though you never meant to trod,
elated and forewarned
you stood knee deep in me.

*Linda Dominique Grosvenor*

## Amoré

New and unrehearsed,
this love of mine,
aching like
a winter chill
to melt with you.
You are my melody
my cafe latté,
my naked trembling lips
a meeting of the minds
every eye beholds you,
my Valentine.

## Showering

The scent of crushed
strawberries and citrus caresses
underneath streams of water
vibrating and massaging, almost too hot.
You slather yourself with something
called *Heaven* from the Gap.
My shower soaked hair
clings to your back,
as you seek a spot where
I've never been kissed.
Moistened lips are a pleasure,
closer, making fantasies
stand up and take notice
as ecstasy flows, down the drain.
Down the drain.

*Linda Dominique Grosvenor*

## Vice

I can recollect when you noticed me
in a somewhat standoffish style,
grazing the core of who I am
as your smile tickled my fancy
and your lips taught mine to kiss.
How dare I say *I love you* first
and shake our picture perfect
love affair by the roots,
and my brutal truth
is only vindicated by
the involuntary words spoken by your silence.
Never once have I denied that yours was
a love I would have died for,
needing you and wanting you,
nothing more, nothing less
honestly I spoke this, surrendering to the sky
and all the while knowing,
your love might be my vice.

## Who

A galaxy of emotions,
the gaggle of our love,
the gnosis of our connection
from a higher cause.
A granule of feeling,
created ostentatious desires,
as a stampede of rationales
were singed by your fire.
Yes my heart does slumber,
for no one else will do,
'cause who will be my Eden?
Or who will be my you?

## Scorched

Passion warm, igniting
that singes the edges of
a p p r e h e n s i o n
and fuel desires within.
You strike me and light me
and coax me from the
confines of complacency,
smirks and smiles of delight
as other recite these words
and ponder our love so tight.
Your lips fan the flames
mine compliantly do the same
daring the rain to extinguish
what's too hot to touch
but burns in you and I forever.

## Flower

Innocently I dangle in the breeze
that pulls back my petals
and exposes my nectar.
The sun confirms that
this is my season
as the heat ripens me
and the skies quench my thirst.
I pose discretely
wanting to be admired
never plucked or uprooted.
You pass my way
filling your nostrils on
the sweetness of my being,
landing in my space
tempting me with the buzzing
of your wings —
and the melody of your song,
promising not to alter my essence,
vowing to never sting me.

## Sugar

I want to speak your mother tongue, fluently
and crumble thick red earth about your feet
so you'd imagine you were back home,
buses humming, lanky youngsters bumming
street vendors pushing off their dusty wares, and me
peeping from tattered curtains near coconut trees
wearing a flimsy sky blue prairie dress,
hoping you'll notice me, between dawn and dusk,
with my bare feet and nervous girlish laughter.
The sun sets and there's still no sign of you
I kneel alone now, wishing we could share some
pungent sweets, I kneel alone now,
silently praying you'll come calling for my sugar.

## Assume

I tried to love you but
just kept missing the mark.
I emptied my emotions into
the hand-carved bowl of your love
and you ate from it.
You over-indulged,
filling yourself on the
cabernet sauvignon of my being.
And just think, you thought I was a child,
you often said I was too young.
You assumed I couldn't make you happy,
you thought my love had no meaning.

## Honey

You bait me with mango lips and
succulent threads chased by the
throaty grumbles that slowly escape,
and I lie helplessly between your
anticipation and hesitation
pondering heaven and you.

## Honeymoon

The midst of joy dampens our faces
no longer caricatures of make believe,
putting away pasts and broken up toys
taking out the tomorrows of our dreams.
Running through lily and poppy fields
naked I stand before you,
the sun is beaming exposing all,
this is our honeymoon.

## Livid

I'm starved for your affection
I'm livid for your love
kiss me and kiss me again
it will never be enough.
I loathe the proper etiquette
of how lovers in public should be,
the warmth of your arms
the softness of your kiss,
they make me.

## Accomplice

Your love is my heart's accomplice
for you are such a gentlemanly bandit
as you ate from cruelty yet spoke of delight.
Spanish eyes that were dreadfully shy
etched love's proof on a tree of forever
in a violent kingdom of men I have
come to adore, and those I seldom favor.

## Joy

If God afforded me the time to love
I would spend every fancy thought
that I had stored to impress you.
I would wear my heart loosely
so it would fall for you, and
I'd fast forward to the scene
where our hearts and minds agree
and the butterflies tap dance
to our sylabellic gymboree.
Your moist lips would linger
making satisfaction commonplace,
and on your passion I would be fed,
for there is no other explanation
that can convey that your love
is my preference.

## Fire

Gleaming in an electric
honey-colored essence
enlightening yet forewarning
of dangers that can destroy.
Jealousy is feverishly evident,
oh how love did enrage him so.
Moving closer to the core of you,
scorched by your pride
or was it the sun? Nights have
drenched my pillow sweet,
and rent my dreams,
rendering them a falsehood.
But my kiss has freed you
from your service,
in parting I must confess
to be a part of your fairytale
I'd purr softly at your feet,
drinking milk from your
savage world of jilted lovers
'til nothing left burns inside me
quite like this love
that has ignited a fire.

## Dreams

Dreams being sent by the wind,
biting the tide, waiting for
the innocence of bravado
to sound the warning bells
and ask the wallflower to dance.
But she's driving fast
and going somewhere that sends
the breeze through her hair
and changes her last name.
A silent war inside herself, she's fighting
though all she really possesses
is the power to surrender.

## Mail

Anxiously waiting, anticipating
the joys that correspondence brings.
It is only the lavender scented
paper with dried lilies impregnated
pressed so purposely with a
love stamp that I am after.
It is more than just words,
for the envelope itself does
my heart no justice, it is the
symbolic gesture of the time
you have taken to share your mind
that sends me spinning.

## Righteous

Our love is righteous; do you know what that means?
Be it true, then we shall nurture
and teach our children of desires and love
not of suffering and plight.
For my heart suffers not at your hand
yet your love isn't free, and it is not mine.
For she holds you captive with trickery and deceit
proving still that chivalry is not dead.
Yet despite your bitterness and unavailability
you love me like a man.
You speak to me softly and whisper
allowing our hearts to linger in a poetic expression.
You are my bridge and I am the water
that runs under it, as your love runs through me.
We are one yet divided, can you understand?
Our love is righteous, you love me like a man.

## Vows

The vows we defy as roaming eyes
make their bed in the comfort of another
and infringe on the face of purity
holding contentment at bay,
drowning hope in the wake of
disbelief and shattered dreams.
Wonders never cease to amaze
as freely I commit myself to be made a fool.
Yet I'd gladly sacrifice my heart
if my heart were your destination,
and I shall fight, for I assume
that love was meant to die for.

## June

I prepare myself with a boarding pass
and strappy heels that invite the contour
of shaven legs to stroll through your mind and wander.
The sun glistens as I pace patiently
shades conspicuously shielding my revealing eyes,
my attire tempting, in its capacity of disclosure
and a magazine camouflaging my nervousness.
I await your embrace as your smile
serves me up a sweet slice of forever
and your lips repeatedly welcome
the remembrance of my voice
as we both agree that we
are too far apart not to be missed
and too close to not be smitten.

## Ambiguity

Your love is ambiguous,
like dancing in a puddle
because you don't want to get wet.
Your silence is screaming "call me"
yet your unused lips never ask for favors.
Requests are too much like needing.
"Go slow," you caution, afraid of the
quickening pace of your own heart.
But I'm immersed in a copy of Love by Buscaglia
because I'm really trying to understand you.
I need to uncover why your mind is free
but your emotions don't dare cop to a lesser plea.

## Real

You want to know
if my love is for real,
you desperately
try to discover.
Deeply penetrating
my earth's core
reeling in the
expression on my face,
calling my name
as I whisper and sigh
in your ear,
giving you all that I am.
Your gentlemanly way
leaves me wanting
and needing more
as you wave good-bye
from the taxi.

## Never

I never touched you
but I know you,
the way your voice commands
me to expose myself
and tell you the
God's honest truth.
I've never seen you but
you are familiar, for I've
touched parts of you
secret, private,
like ever common déjà vu.
My empty arms
they have never
embraced your shoulders, your face
yet I can mimic your strength
because it never lies or compromises.
Like a fluid melody that ends too soon
I am and we are because
I know you and your love,
although I never.

## Skin

I invite in my skin
to advocate for
the butterflies
who have their way with me.
I kneel at nervous laughter
that dares me to submit
for the love of a country,
love of a man,
for the love of me.

## Naked

Laying peeled down nude
wrapped in the loveliness of words
that join us delicately like commas
describe us like adjectives
and move us like verbs.
Lips greeting, thighs meeting
the scent of you creeps in me.
Body convincing love will do,
hands assuming the rest of you
would reaffirm and give in too.
I'm shivering defenseless now,
goose bumps abound, as I vow
to never vacate this comfort of bliss.
Knowing not your heart's refrain
my love will yet remain the same
only the seasons will change —
I promise you, in the nude.

## When

Eyes wide open I think of you,
my thoughts race to the finish line
as we wade in this love so deep.
When can I see you?
You hold out, withdraw hesitantly —
arms folded, daring me to
presumptuously make the first move.
Don't you call my name
at night just to hear it echo
in the confines of your sheets?
In your bedroom as you sleep?
Don't you nuzzle your pillow
pretending its softness is me?
Patiently I'm waiting for you
to wake and love me like a fairytale.
Come make my mornings love
drink me as you read the news
make me a ritual you can't undo
clothe me with your soul's tattoo
help me push up the sun.

## Gypsy

If you were willing to tackle me
I could love you like a gypsy.
I'd be hell bent on redeeming you
and unearthing your fallacies
waving them good-bye
from my covered wagon.
Or nibbling toast cautiously behind
the makeshift frank stand by the bay
in the glistening noonday sun,
my reflection lathering you twice
and mentally dining teeth first into
the succulent truth that is by far
lovelier still.

## Hot

Like a chili pepper I'm hot for you
nothing can quench it, decrease it
or remotely comfort my tongue.
As my legs hug you, telling you
don't go, begging you to stay awhile,
or at least until morning.
Your arms say "no this is too hard for me."
Your heart interrupts telling mine,
"ignore them, they are only arms
though they embrace you needingly
sometimes they lie like lips on fire."

## Linger

If you decided that tomorrow
was too much for you to offer
and that today just about satisfied
your yesterday, I'd be cool with that,
or I'd try my best to pretend to be.
I'd turn my head so you wouldn't see my tears,
or see my lips tremble. I'd never want you
to be able to tell that you got under my skin
and that I needed you and made plans for us
that included vacations, Valentine's Day
and our names on Christmas cards.
If you said that you needed newer and less intense
and that wasn't me, and that you wanted
to go cold turkey, I'd stop calling you
if you asked me to. I'd pretend that every time
I heard my phone ring that I didn't hope it was you.
I'd get over you eventually —
I suppose. I'd live off of memories, old conversations
and love letters, unimpressed by the fact
that you didn't understand that love lingers.

## Sea

Your heart vows not to love me as
morning comes too soon and tepid winds toss
like waves running from the sea.
I dare thee to banish thoughts of me
like footprints left on the shores of
someone seeking aesthetic conversation
only to have it orally pacify you
like hearts beating in tandem
all evidence erased by the rising tide.

## Celebrate

I skinned my knee in a slippery courtyard
with thorns and briar afoot
I vowed I wouldn't fall for you,
but I ran to save myself I suppose.
My contrite persona, runny nose
as I perch my knowledge of you
on the swing of a gilded cage.
You mirror gray studded clouds
evaporating in urban decay
as love transcends culture, me,
and you eat frozen fruit
soaked in champagne to
confirm my fleeting thoughts and
celebrate my hearts perfect landing.

## Matilda

"I crave her," he says.
She has the most amazing lips,
I love kissing them.
And though I believe it's true
for him to say —
that no one has ever stimulated
his mind, body and soul
more and more than she,
I know that being adored
and coveted in such a sincere
and faithful fashion
is as close to heaven
as we will get,
without our feet
leaving the ground.

## She

She adores him
like her daily ration
her ear hugging his lips
that from a distance
do amazing things
of little value to eavesdroppers.

## Extricate

I try to extricate my heart
from your finger's grasp and guard it
like a well armed Roman general
against your tongue's reputation.
Your verbal intimacy told me
secrets of an esoteric love affair
that gossiped on every street corner
and I stored your confessions
in a cinnabar box with potpourri,
because your truth is too fragrant
to be overlooked, and your passion
is so heavy, I can't help but fall for you.

## Dance

I dance fast, alone
stopping only when
the music ceases
applauding me,
and the weather exists
indecisive, I swivel hips
my smile engaged,
as Marc Anthony
serenades me
in my natural habitat.

## Sunrise

Love me slowly like a hot Texas sunrise
that steals the seconds morning dew
left behind, weeping goodbye night.

## Taxicab

Your lips and my hips, throbbing
groping up passion's dark stairwell
misdirecting traffic, getting lost
in the synchronized motion
of our tongue's fire, and its flames
that cleave to the increased yearning,
clinging tightly, deeper, licking your
famished heart's interior, discretely
fondling your interest, as you beg
slowly and softly in my ear to
pay our surroundings no attention.

## Autumn

Spent maple leaves
rained down on me today
like the thick legs of summer
that bid him farewell.

## Introverted

My weary eyes are laden
like a diseased tree that bears no fruit.
Who will come to water me?
Deem me worthy of a liaison
not always shrouded in secrecy?
Instead they bide my time and
their interest lies, avoiding commitment
like superstitious sidewalk cracks.

### Sleeping

Your beauty is a habit
making my vagabond heart
through light and mysteries
slay itself like burnt offerings.

## Easy

You push my buttons; undress me flimsy
and walk me like a mangy mutt
lost in the shadow of those who came before you,
ignoring my purpose, shelling my heart
like the hot back of a female crab
as I normally use these arms to
clothe you like a child soaking wet
from the rain, hurrying home for the
nurture of warmth that comforts
a lying thick tongue that can't
wait to brag and tell his friends I'm easy.

## Falling

I drink you in like orange footprint across the sky
though I've never been loved only underfed, mistreated,
so, I assume you'll leave too and I
mumble an inaudible departure
a generic adios, a solitary goodbye it seems
as the autumn leaves drop off the trees
and I fall for you too,
only not as lightly or as colorfully.

## Uncovered

In this snow blanketed circumstance
I can uncover you like the spring's thaw
fertilizing you with budding possibilities.
In our telephone etiquette
we toy with nouns and pronouns
as you sit safe in your crush velvet style
and I reel in the synchronized memory of your lips.
I ask you bluntly "do friends kiss?"
You say "more than they should,
sometimes not often enough."
"Are you serious?" I ask,
you say "love is measured in degrees..."
"Yeah? And?"
"Right now we're at 350 degrees
and getting hotter," you say.
While I smirk to myself having a flashback
blushing, thinking, "yeah, I know."

## Alibi

I don't need a cover to love you
as white filmy train stations
leave the residue of winter's crunchy salt behind
I grab you fist first snuggling closer to the wooly frolic
to you, your scent and your warmth
as your breath visibly escapes you.
Closer than the remote control,
I step over your imaginary line
changing channels to something we both enjoy.
But some take pleasure in, others disdain
for our display, our exaggerated goodbye
but none of this matters,
only your chilly lips, my cheek,
your frozen fingers, my waist
and the promise of next week,
as you sprint for your downtown train.

## Wasted

My love was shaken and wasted
on hands that cleave to mother's breast
bruising nipples and nursing still
trembling and afraid to let go
except for an occasional day trip
where he'd pick virgin cherries
discarding their seed and stem, uselessly.
Like a dead fish he engaged me
shiny, scaly and sometimes avoiding
tugging and thrashing on tourists lure
appropriately smelling of lies all the while.

## Abstract

High maintenance, costly confusion
I warned you before your first felt tipped drag
I'd have you coming, going and fumbling
trying to make a quadrilateral equation of us
calling, wondering and avoiding my machine
contemplating nervously a makeshift future
where time wasn't just an ominous tick
but a flick of my hip and a lovely puff
on something that might kill you dead
if you don't hold on tight and master it.

## Remember

At a deserted bus station
in a strange town
near a forgotten moment
the song says, "Love is Strange"
and you agree grinning at me with
ferocious teeth, squinting at
light skinned teenage girls in
fuchsia shantung mini skirts
and white patent leather go-go boots
who smoke cheap fashionable cigars,
sing blue haikus as the sun rises
and splits the sky pink and blue.
It's pathetic how I become invisible
in the presence of them all and
stir not even a whimsical fancy as
your eyes assist them with their journey
and I carry my own bags.

## More

Kissing you makes me want you more
wholly, infinitely and unchanging
as your tongue opens parts of me
forbidden, hidden, special,
buried under layers of indelibly etched
circumstantial evidence.
But how can my mind cleave, grieve, receive
where your heart needs to be, pleased
and you not feel a blessed thing?
Like the tiny earthquakes trembling through me,
when I melt into your intellectual symphony
and you unknowingly make me want you
all the more.

## Everything

When I say you are my everything
that means complete, finished and done.
There is nothing to add and nothing to take away.
No one can dissolve or infringe upon it,
it is perfect even in its imperfect state,
for it is ours emotionally, mentally and physically.
When I fell for you I can recall,
my heart was wakened by the wind,
breathing the breath of life
on a dying being that was me.
Aching and yearning for a love
that was completely mine,
my famished heart has been fed,
and had brought me to this place
where the zephyr breeze and warm sand
invite me to coo on an long distance call.
It is you, fate has revealed to my soul,
it was always you.

## Chores

In between the tediousness
of my daily chores
I find the time to tell you
with words how I adore,
your presence and your beauty
your feelings and your touch
your lips and how they greet me,
I thank you very much.

## Naught

If my love was unfaithful
I would not mind so,
if my love was immortal
I would not die so,
if my love was not caring
I would not hurt so,
if my love were not
nor would we, and then know I
would cease to be.

## Jealousy

Jealousy it eats you up
gnaws you deep
robs your soul.
Jealousy stirs the fire
tricks the mind
and takes its toll.
Jealousy is a slow decay
that builds apprehensions
instead of truth,
jealousy isn't worth the risk
of living without you.

## Jessy

A full time daydreamer
closes her eyes and kisses in French.
She loves like a child
unaware of the envy,
hasn't learned to cry when she's happy
or sing when she's blue.
A lyricist with peach fuzz
a little dusty fairytale
with a snowflaked tongue
and commitment shy mind.
Pulling petals off daisies
dried leaves underfoot,
rolling downhill past a
"*no trespassing*" sign
Oh, how she loves the grass!
Oh, how she loves you!

## Forbidden

The way we kiss the way we touch
should not our love be forbidden?
What mere words can describe
this heart that was so thoughtfully hidden?
What love is this that I shall feel
so greater than I've ever known?
Will it depths be eternal bliss?
Or will it rob my soul?
As I ponder the unforeseen,
I turn and find you standing there,
rescue me lest I shall fall
victim to my fears.

## If

If I had but one chance
to show you my eternal flame,
and the torch that I carry
that bridges our love
then it would not be a secret
on contemplating and pondering
but there would be compliance
and submission because
you understood.

## Leaves

Like fallen leaves my love has bad timing
leaving you exposed and shivering
in the afterthought of my affection.
My emotions build you to this hierarchal plateau
where others can only imagine your needs yet
my impulse is to drown you in delicacies of
love sonnets with mushy dedications,
and blush at your impromptu marriage proposal
in a crowded café.

## Midnight

Candle wax, bubble bath, laughing in the aftermath
of your unbridled affection as it oozes between me,
my fingers, 10 toes, two lips and shapely hips,
making its way down to the chorus line of my
superlative of likes, which includes your hands,
your moist lips, and a wealth of discovery in between.

## Rain

I want to stand with you in the rain
pellets of a drenching downpour
as we melt together in the mud
and chase old suspicions that
no l o n g e r exist
except in the minds of those
who have nothing because
they chose to give nothing.
I want to remember your love
as excessive, especially when
you give all of your passion to me
spending every royal drop
saving not an ounce for yourself
because you have mine in reserve.

## Always

To me it seems
that I want more than dreams,
so kiss my soul and I'll touch the stars
as they dance in unison
blessing the languid sky with laughter
as I give you my heart
until death or life ever after,
if always isn't far enough.

## Sinful

My love for you isn't sinful
as I fall forward in your rhapsody
intoxicated by your presence
and pleased as your tongue speaks words
that like a spell bring magic to my life.
I don't believe in karma or psychics
but I believe in your love
because it tiptoed and caught me
unaware and unarmed as it bathed me
in this predestined expectancy.

## Could

I could have loved you
for the Vera Wang and
the Tiffany solitaire
I could have married you
pretending my desire for him
had been voided by his exit.
I could have seen the dust
and pretend that it had settled
everything that came before you and I.
I could have sworn my heart
to secrecy and blindfold it
when thoughts of him tried to
creep and soothe me in the humid night.
I could have coped after awhile,
letting go of his shadowy memory
with both hands, assuming we were
no longer magnets joined in the
negative and positive of our attraction,
assuming we were no longer destiny
I could have soothed my conscious
in the drying of your tears and the
beating of your heart on mine when you said
"go if you must, Dominique, just come back to me."

## Fallen

You know the words to my favorite song
we talk til 3am on a humid night in June
they say I've fallen but I don't know
it's more like losing altitude
I close my eyes and I can hear you speak
your pause, your hesitation
6am the phone rings and I pray it's you
pay for 6 days and the Sunday paper is free
it's only the Daily News.
I asked Moma if I could keep you
she said, only if you'd agree to stay
"love is a two-way street *dear girl*," s he offered
as your gravitational pull lures me
and has me fearlessly obeying
your honey-suckle lips pursed in passion
and what they desire to do to me.

## Perfection

"Surely not me," he said
with his crooked smile
and sea green eyes
pondering my purpose
for rendering him in a poem.
Specks of freckles, button nose
lips slightly pale from
lack of sunlight and love,
I don't mince words
I delight in expression
every lover, every tear
blanketed in this verse,
the fear of feeling does
not wait for us to digest it
when you love someone
they are perfect.

## Suppose

Like leading a horse to water
will you drink from my heart?
For I am unchartered territory my love
and more than just a nibble I offer
as I invite you to dine on the
endless thoughts of my mind.
Come chase away the butterflies
as your touch prompts my love to bloom
and I beckon solace to ravish me.
Somewhat reserved, you observe
being the woman that I am,
yet, in a stolen moment I'm not afraid to say
forever, only you can love me as I'm
thinking of you by the beautiful moonlight.

## Yearn

Your love feels good against my nakedness
and I share the delight you evoke with a smile,
my yearning love meets the need of you
my legs draw you closer in a moment
where our hips press as do we face to face
and within a fraction of an inch our lips meet
then adamantly protest a hasty departure.
Your words fill me, loving me in second languages
you entice me with the flashes of a silent epiphany
you deliver me repeatedly in an unchanging melody
where your residue is left all over me and the light
that dances in yours eyes never says goodbye
yet leaves me blushing in a moment that
only God could have predicted.

## Kid

If I could see inside your mellow heart
sneak a peek, peering and reaching deep down
to the central core, would I find Hot Wheels there?
Or the hidden confession that you
still watch Saturday morning cartoons?

## Facade

He's haunted by a facade
she's elusively the devil,
an aura of his delight
fastening herself to his heart
keeping in sync, sort of.
Her claws of possession
dig deeper, reaching the lifeline
or something somewhat vital,
a macabre hellion
henceforth Helter Skelter
persuading him in no uncertain terms
that he should be hers.

## Caught

6 a.m., tangled hair and wrinkled bedsheets
I wake still elated but you're not there,
not a residue of what we've shared,
not a morsel of unfettered affection
to nudge me on into my hectic day,
only space, distance and brief email
that makes me want to run across the 4 states
that separate me from you and futilely
push New York closer to the Carolinas.
This is my cloud, you put me here to bask
like a nude sunbather oblivious to eyes
that try and tell me I'm naked although
I'm wearing you. Your love caught me,
like a creative tongue with no limits
noisily licking and thoroughly bathing me.
6:37 a.m. I won't budge, here I lie, still yours,
realizing there's never a dull moment
with my urgent thoughts of you.

## Spanish

I want to love you in Spanish
not just villas in Madrid
or fiestas and sombreros
but I want to say my favorite things out loud
and relish your lips as they chuckle and
repeat after me as I mispronounce words
I never had the nerve to say in English.

## Friday

Let your love for me overflow
but don't you dare make me cry
come closer but don't let our hands touch
only the lingering expression of our lips.
Remember Friday? When we were sitting
on the sofa leaning into the newness of pleasure?
I want to always kiss you like that, because
you say, "the novelty of passion is spontaneity,"
and on a parched Friday night with no outlet
for my overzealous love, I can really dig that.

## Born

"I was born to kiss you," she said
"your heart is all I'm after."
"This if forever isn't it?" she asked,
masking tears with laughter.
Escaping delusions of grandeur she called it
perfecting the vision of us,
on a sentimental journey she declared
"I'm not naked, I'm in love."

## Baby

I wanna make a baby with you, a boy and a girl
she'll have my sass and he'll have your eyes
and when she smiles playing head tag with your
mind, you'll say, "you're just like your Moma."
But see I want their need to be birthed from
the core of love and offering and we must agree
to never use them as a bargaining chip
shuffled back and forth through baggage laden
weekend visitations for greater gain or allow them
to belittle us both in a sitcom rerun scenario
where he plays you against me and she can't stop
telling your new girlfriend she's pretty.

## King

You stepped into my light and lifted my dark shades
revealing the hard me that needed to be
to get along on these dirty vindictive streets,
I tried to be nonchalant and make you figure
I could take or leave your love but inside
I was crouched down nodding on the rush of you.
You made me tap myself pumping adrenaline,
raising my lazy thin veins to the surface,
you make me forgo my next microwave meal
as I fed myself on your unrehearsed tongue
that lured me into a repeated submission. And you
yeah it was you who made my memories of
those other brothers a fallacy as you rode into
my lackluster world on the white horse and left
a diamond studded trail for me to find my way
back to you, for you, to be with you , only you baby
so I crown you, yeah I crown you, 'cause your love is
king.

## Magnets # 3

His symphony plays like a thousand bare moon petals
always wanting to smear her luscious fluffy place
please be still as two frantic lovers moan and shake
so, in a delirious misty summer rain and ache like a whisper
asking to scream in eternity.

## Music

You draped your love across my conscious
you sustained my crescendo beckoning
as light falls like metallic rain on my mind
you cradled me in the treble of your affection
making me oh, so glad we both came.

## Armed

Your love is my heart's only weapon,
it binds me and sets me free
unscathed yet left to wander
in the everafter of us.

## Truth

Your heart held the single truth
confessing little, denying all else,
you cover me completely
laughter, always laughing.

## Being

Being a poet
is a lot like being naked,
exposing yourself
and flashing someone
occasionally.
Let me be your poet,
I'll dress you with the
raiment of my youth
and expose my big dreams
with simple meanings
as you cover me
in words that go together
but don't necessarily have to rhyme.

## Misunderstood

A simple misunderstanding
a play on words, a twist of fate,
it's not the person, in fact
it's love we overestimate.
For who knows who you are
one day laughing, the next day crying,
frugal is an understatement
emotionlessly dying.

## Yesterday

Yesterday I looked at you
and I envisioned what we could be,
in the night on the phone
are you all alone? You say things
to me that your heart believes.
Mountains, oceans, sunsets and
full moons, you make me smile
for a little while, oh yeah,
I forgot, cartoons!

## Rejection

My heart is a flood waiting to happen
a seed in the Spring time about to bloom
the power of beauty is bittersweet
alone in the shadows but still quite you.
Your scent left on my pillow
our kisses weren't make believe,
secrets and broken promises
as you claim to love me.

**Free**

A look of confusion on your face
as I set you free,
friendship is what I offer
for your mind did wander
and your heart preoccupied foolishly.

## Ransom

My faithfulness undying,
reserve is seldom spent
should I defend my honor,
if this love is heaven sent?
The beauty of time escapes us,
prompted by this hidden tree
on your love I will casually call,
'twas mean to be.
Your interest compliments me
beckoning the further sounding doves,
the unequivocal facets of love
plenitude and bliss
a penny for your thoughts,
and a ransom for a kiss.

## Toy

Running right away
deflowered, dethroned
the frost of never
covers our love now
as you have revealed
the deceptive nature of man.
Such a liar, I suppose
yet, it is in us all to be unkind
so I, the woman, seek to be unchained
and seek a new bridge
for my love to run under.
And you, the man
are rummaging through the trash
trying to fix our love
like a broken toy —
though you never cared about it
when it was new.

## Seventeen

Eyes closed, head back
your palms on the curve of my hips
it all reminds me of seventeen.
I was a novice then,
wondering why love wasn't convenient
or as predictable as I normally am.

## Coffee

I put my lips to you
and taste your strength
diluted with heavy cream
that never leaves you weak,
and the sweetness of you on my tongue
is not remotely feminine,
as I gulp you by the mouthful,
and savor the flavor that is in fact
delicious enough to deter your bitterness.

## Ode to Tim

Thick lips, wide curvaceous hips
you ran from my love saying that it burned you
deep like a ferocious fire,
you acted like it chased you
and followed you every day on your way home
then you call me on the phone late at night
saying you missed me awfully bad
you begged me to come back and stay
telling me I can make your heart my home
then in the next breath you say my love
makes you uncomfortable to be you
without being judged for what I want you to be.
Since you didn't know what I was thinking
you took an uneducated guess
but I'm not complexed really
all that was on my mind was
playing by the rules, being true,
allowing you to do what you do
so I wouldn't be blue...I loved you.

Linda Dominique Grosvenor is the author of several novels. She's also a poet and aspiring filmmaker that currently resides in North Carolina with her husband John who publishes a literary magazine called Rhapsody (rhapsodyinblack.com) You can visit her cyberworld at:

**www.lindadominiquegrosvenor.com**